Patrick Cudmore

Cudmore's Prophecy o the Twentieth Century

Patrick Cudmore

Cudmore's Prophecy o the Twentieth Century

ISBN/EAN: 9783741191282

Manufactured in Europe, USA, Canada, Australia, Japa

Cover: Foto ©ninafisch / pixelio.de

Manufactured and distributed by brebook publishing software
(www.brebook.com)

Patrick Cudmore

Cudmore's Prophecy o the Twentieth Century

CUDMORE'S
Prophesy of the Twentieth Century

BY

P. CUDMORE, Esq., B. H.,

Counselor at Law,

Author of the "Irish Republic," "The Civil Government of the States'
and "Constitutional History of the United States," "Poems and
Songs," and "Buchanan's Conspiracy," "The Nicaragua
Canal and Reciprocity," "The Battle of Clontarf,"
and "Cleveland's Maladministration," etc.

PRICE, 10 CENTS.

NEW YORK:
For sale by P. J. Kenedy, No. 5 Barclay Street.
1899.

CUDMORE'S

PROPHECY

OF THE

TWENTIETH CENTURY.

The despot's power and the despot's rod,
Oppress'd the people in the name of God!
The people, like sheep, in flocks were driven
By the tyrants, who claimed a right from heaven;
Churchmen often from th' pulpit did preach,
A curse on free thought and on free speech.
The people oft, for opinion's sake,
By tyrants were burned at the stake; .
And the prophets, who for the truth long stood,
Sealed their opinion with their precious blood.
For conscience's sake—alack! alack!—
Thousands and thousands suffered on th' rack!
By lying fallacies from Pluto's den
Bigots enslav'd the minds of men.
It was a great crime to differ in creed;
Then men were burned if they disagreed!
In church and state the song was obedience;
Legal sages cried, "Order and allegiance."
Not allegiance to God and to man's rights,

But to the despot's power—brutal might!
Poets who sung the divine rights of man,
Tyrants and bigots put them under ban.
And the weak before the strong did fall,
The unjust the just did then enthrall!
What vile oppression, what base cruelty,
Was inflicted on poor humanity!
Woe to the vanquished after th' battle—
Men were bought and sold like brute cattle.
Kings and nobles made and broke the law;
Law was an engine the poor to awe.
The law's engines, the gibbet, jail and rack,
Forced the people to pay a load of tax.
In those dark ages, the man of free mind
In some dark dungeon was confined.
Judges cared not for wrong or right,
But the king's "order;" for then th' sword was might.
And the people were driven like cattle,
To fight for nobles and kings in battle—
They should aid the king in all his strife,
But should not ask if the king was right.
Great was the lords' and the bigots' arrogance
O'er the people sunk in ignorance!
But now the world has an aspect bright.
Oh! behold free thought—heavenly right.
And soon free thought from learning's holy well
Ignorance and bigotry will dispel.
Bigotry will meet its doom—its just fate—
For the church will divorce from the state.
Grand will be the light of liberty
In the free twentieth century.
In that age tyranny will decline
Before free speech and freedom of the mind.
The world's opinion no more will jar,
Science will be the bright, prevailing star;
Reason, justice and truth will be man's guide;

Public opinion will rule wrong and right.
By science great battles will be fought,
And by the noble army of free thought.
The blighting power of despotism
Will yield to truth—individualism.
It will not be heresy or treason
To use free judgment—God's gift, reason!
Then every nationality
Will assert individuality.
Oh! Mammon's sons, great will be your greed
For gold, and plunder will be your creed.
For God and religion you will lose awe,
Your only fear, the hangman and the law.
They will follow ev'ry vile excess;
Their sefish motto will be, "Success."
From vice th' people will be effeminate,
Each generation will be more degenerate.
And those whose sires fought for liberty
Will sink into low depravity.
Avarice the human heart will sink,
And mighty will be the dollar's clink.
Wealth, pride and fashion, like a vast flood,
Will drown all thoughts of the public good.
Justice and truth will be call'd sedition
By those whose god is lucre and ambition.
The people, sons of the brave and free,
Will sink to base, brutal slavery;
Not the slavery where man is sold,
But to Avarice and Mammon's gold!
In that age will be poverty and crime
Among the people of every clime.
Mammon's creed will cause great penury,
Villainy, shame and misery.
The world will decline in hospitality;
Then will vanish love and generosity.
Though the world shall appear a carnal den,

There will always be just and moral men.
Millions 'll sink in the mire of dishonesty,
Still there will be justice, truth, morality.
There will be but little piety,
But fraud, doubt and infidelity.
Selfishness will affect all nations;
The rich will disown their poor relations;
Youths and maidens will be unblushing—bold,—
And relations will be as strangers, cold.
Th' people's idol will be power and pelf,
And man will be a law unto himself.
In that age of luxury and greed,
Charity will fly from ev'ry creed;
In that age of learning and progression,
Will be fraud, cunning and deception;
And man will be hard-hearted and near,
And stiff-necked as the colt and steer.
Alas! in every clime and nation
Th' people will lack true adoration—
For th' clergy the people will lose awe;
Their only dread will be shame and law.
Church authority millions will reject,
And the clergy will meet with dire neglect.
Church yards and temples will then decay,
The clergy will get but scanty pay;
Temples will be doom'd to confiscation,
And holy things to vile desecration.
The rule in the coming generation,
Self will and insubordination.
Great will be the people's pomp and pride;
Honest poverty they will deride;
The people will be refined—wise they'll talk,—
But they will be too indolent to walk!
To gain wealth will be the venal rage,
Th' rich will be honored more than the sage.
In that selfish and degenerate day.
Youth will have no respect for age;

There will be jealousy and much strife
Between child, parent, husband and wife!
In that degenerate age of woe,
You will not know friend from foe!
Sad age—man his fellow man won't trust,—
Each generation will be more unjust.
Youth in health and vigor will decline,
And will be more and more prone to crime.
Men will be like angels—intellectually,—
But they will be like demons in dishonesty.
Kings will be hurled from their station,
A republic will be in ev'ry nation;
Powers, thrones, titles and all such sham
Will yield to the divine rights of man.
Nobility, titles and monarchy
Will be overthown by democracy.
Kings will imbrue their hands in human blood,
They will be unjust and practice falsehood.
To do justice, rulers will be loth;
They will care little for word or oath!
Summer in winter, winter in spring,
England will have neither queen nor king.
To fight for kings will be high treason—
Th' people will be rul'd by right—reason.
Kings, potentates will cry demagogism;
They can't resist the tide of liberalism.
There will be great clamor and mighty strife
Till th' people gain equal civil rights.
There will be the right civilization—
Unlimited, glorious, toleration!
There will be in every nation
Complete religious toleration!
Then the church will feel persecution.
The clergy will live in destitution.
It is a question of nicety,
What is the import of liberty.

It means that you may do what you please;
Ah! but your neighbors you must not tease.
Liberty is God's gift, heavenly bright;
Thou shalt not encroach on your neighbor's right.
He is a fool or bigot who would mourn
For th' dark ages that ne'er will return!
The money changers—th' Jews—Christ did purge
From God's temple with His wrath and scourge.
Usurious Jews from Palestine did fly,
And settled beneath Italy's fair sky.
Th' year eight hundred in Italian land
The Lombard Jews started the first bank.
Fair Venice's merchant princes—not a few—
Were under tribute to the Shylock Jew!
The Shylock's pandemonium bands
Invented interest gold-bearing bonds,
And mortgages, the French, for death's grip or grasp—
Instruments that hold millions in th' Jews' clasp.
Shylocks, Shylocks—the usurious knaves—
With interest bonds have made men slaves.
Eight hundred of the era of Christ's creed,
The Jews then settled in Lombard street.
There they ply their vile, usurious trade,
Both kings and people now they enslave.
In Lombard street not far from th' Strand,
There stands Mammon's temple—England's bank.
There the usurious daily ply their trade,
And shave the world without a barber's blade.
The curse of nations, worse than war and pest,
Is Satan's-invention—the public debt!
The Shylocks—a usurious crew—
Made England the paradise of Jews.
Rothschilds, bankers,—the vile money rings—
Have their heels upon the necks of kings!
The usurers the people doth enthrall;
They've a voice in making peace and war.
Shylock, Shylock, with a heart of steel,

Little he recks for the public weal;
How little he cares for tribute and tax;
Well he knows how to fill his money bag.
The tax on all civilized nations
Is the Shylock's field for speculations!

In that age of speculation and rings,
Great monopolists and railroad kings,
To make a fortune, either right or wrong,
Is all fair play with the venal throng;
And in Wall Street is great Mammon's shrine;
Fraud and plunder is not held a crime.
And to Wall Street to th' bankers and brokers
All will run, except the honest Quakers.
There will be gambling in wheat and oats,
In railroad stocks and in bankers' notes;
There will be gambling in beef and swine;
Gambling will be the passion of th' times.
Alas! that the people of this great nation
Should be so monkey-like in imitation;
And foreign style will then be the fashion,
To ape English lords will be the passion;
And foolish dudes, both old and young,
How they'll lisp and drawl the Cockney tongue.
Purse-proud maidens love noble quality,
A beggar husband with a pedigree;
Then the codfish snobs will have a craze,
To wine and dine lords will be the rage.
On titled drones they'll fawn and flatter,
Like monkeys with grimace and chatter!
They'll try to catch a lord or rotten peer,
Who'll pay them back with laughter and jeer.
And of the fashions let me say a word,
If not out of place, nor yet absurd.
The sons of Mammon will be toil and care
To build great fortunes for a thankless heir!

For spendthrift rakes of the gambling hell;
With distend'd pride mothers' hearts will swell.
And while daughters daily grow like graces,
Overwork'd parents daily have long faces;
And while counting o'er their empty purses,
On the world's fashions shower their curses.
Of freedom the people will proudly boast,
And of the widsom of the laws and courts;
Small rogues will be punish'd, as they ought to be,
While great defaulters will go scot free.
By the laws to prison none will send them,
If they have money to defend them;
And on men's word how few will then rely,
For their word will be a business lie!
To keep their word how little will they care,
Unless it brings them immediate gain.
There will be an age of selfishness, not love,
And filial respect will fly to the realms above.
Then young men will use the meanest slang;
They'll ne'er say "father," but "the old man."
Lax will be the government of the youth,
The people then will face the naked truth
That the people's morals are growing bad—
In the school room they must use the rod.

Then the rage will be high education;
Youth will not work—there will be vexation!
College dudes will either starve or shirk
Before they will toil at manual work!
They will be all style, fashion and parade;
They could do better at some useful trade,
But their fond mothers want to be genteel
And want their children held in high esteem.
Silly mothers and their daughters fair,
How they'll plan to catch some wealthy heir;
He may be a fool or a silly snob,

It matters not, if he has got the cash;
Let him be old, blind, ugly and lame,
If he has the money he's their game.
He can have a beauty any day in marriage,
If he has a fine house and a stylish carriage.
He may be a boor as ugly as sin,
It matters not if he has got the tin!
A business man leads a weary life,
If he has a proud and stylish wife.
She'll call her husband a mean, old sinner,
Unless he gives a grand ball and dinner.
She will call him an old boor and mean clown,
Unless he invites th' snobs of half the town.
The Scriptures say that women must not teach,
But they have always claimed the right to preach.
In this country women yet will rule,
And spank young boys in the public school;
And school mar'ms in bangs, bustles and tights,
Will teach young lords what is woman's rights.
And when young lads take a fit of mirth,
On their backs they'll ply the cane and whip.
They will become pert and very bold—
And if an old maid—a shrew and scold.
How she will try to capture a nice young man,
Or a rich simpleton, surely that is her plan.
Our grandmothers danced both jigs and reels,
Now smart women ride in the streets on wheels;
Our grandmothers sure would faint with fright
Should they see women ride on wheels in tights!
Men will get frightened at th' thought of marriage,
When thinking of a wife, house and carriage,
Parties, balls, divorce courts, domestic strife,
Which make bachelors lead a single life.
From family jars and irritation,
Marriage will yet become a failure!
Grumbling, growling and domestic strife

Will surely end the marriage life.
Then marriage a mere contract will be,
And man will then have the right to go free!
A woman-man—an educated fool—
Has a new fad in the public school.
This silly man introduced this fad;
People say that he has now gone mad!
Our grandmothers would have a fit of glee
At seeing children write 'ere they knew A, B, C.
In th' public schools will be many fads,
And educators will yet go mad!
In the public schools is much stuffing,
And children are blind from much studying!
Professor Andrews may rant and rave,
In a mad house he should have a cage.

Men will degenerate in size and shape,
They will look like the monkey or the ape.
Degenerate youth, say what you can,
Will resemble th' monkey more than man.
Wealth will beget luxury and ease,
The Epicureans will be hard to please.
A robust man will be hard to find;
Men will be feeble in body and mind.
In body and mind men will then decay;
They will be cut off by disease and plague;
And an age of dwarfs—burlesques of man—
As if nature had changed her plan.
They will be old at thirty—horrid frights—
They will wear glasses—all will be purblind.
And in England Cromwell's ghost will rule,
England's House of Lords will meet its doom;
For it is written in th' book of fate
That in England will end church and state.
Then the church, alas! for Episcopalians,
Will yet be plundered by the Cromwellians.

In England will be war, devastation,
Famine, plague and great conflagration.
Then modern Babylon will burn down;
Woe! Woe! to great Sodom—London town!
Then the people will be fierce and mad,
Little they'll care for religion and God!
Then London mob, a fierce, lawless crew,
Will rob and murder the Shylock Jew.
Kings and lords and religion they will deride,
And all kinds of property they will divide;
And great Mammon's temple—London bank—
London rabble will plunder and sack.
England's trade will come to devastation;
Woe! Woe! to the proud British nation.
England, England the nations did enthrall,
Like Babylon and Rome she will fall,
Not by vandals—that lawless crew—
But from workshops, colleges and schools.
War, famine, plague and devastation
Will cause great mountains of taxation!
Tax, oppression, war, speculation
Will cause bankrupts and repudiation.
The British law and constitution
Will be abolish'd by revolution;
And war will rage between the classes,
And the victors will be the masses.
They will rebel against big taxes,
Which will be overthrown by the masses!
There will be no tax for knaves and fools,
And just a little for the public schools.
The common law—that great, cumbrous lore—
Will become obsolete evermore.
A wise and just civilization
Will end monopoly and corporation!
Gambling, cheating and combinations
Will be punished as high treason!

In this country women soon will rule,
In camps and barracks as in the school.
Termagants, their power will be great;
They will rule the churches and the state!
In America will be an oligarchy;
There will be civil war and anarchy.
There will come an age of anarchism,
Which will be followed by barbarism.
Americans will find, when too late,
Th' English fleet thundering at their gate;
And Americans, who in Saxons trust,
Will find when too late their bubble burst.
• The Saxon nation will come to grief;
Behold the wreck of the British fleet!
There will be rejoicing from pole to pole,
When the British empire will be no more.
Th' flags of all nations will be unfurl'd;
She'll have one foe, and that foe the world!

Tribute, taxes and "exactation"
Will be the curse of the Yankee nation!
Churches and churchmen—institutions,
Will receive scanty contributions.
Shylocks, Shylocks, there will come a time
When interest-money will be a crime!
Greedy Shylocks, the world soon will rule;
With trusts and bonds—invention of Jews—
The chains of usurers will be riven,
And all kinds of debts will be forgiven!
A civil war, and the fierce masses
Will abolish tribute, tithes and taxes.
There will come a day of retribution,
And the fiercest Jewish persecution.
What great rejoicing from pole to pole,
   Th' reign of usurers will be no more.
Then rogues and thieves will come to grief,

And trials in the court will then be brief.
He who is convicted of a crime
Will surely receive the "cat-o'-nine."
A time will come of little faith and truth,
And man will be lower than the brute.
In that age the people will revoke
Th' bastinado and the whipping post.
In an age of luxury and ease,
Men will perish of plague and disease;
The people will be luxurious and vain;
Patriotism will be power and gain.
Machines will cause dire destitution,
Avarice, crime, famine—revolution.
Woe! Woe! to the Yankee nation
From food and drink adulteration!
Tobacco, rum, gum-preparation
Will make this a drug-drinking nation.
Columbia will embark in foreign wars,
The soldiers will be the arbiters of th' laws.
There will be scheming and corruption,
The soldiers will control th' elections;
Offices and titles will be bought and sold;
The greatest power will be gold, gold.
In that corrupt age of militarism
The republic will be an imperialism;
In Columbia a band of traitors
Will sell the freedom of the nation.
Knaves, fools, apes and the money ring
Will conspire to make a knave a king!
The Anglo-American combination
Will be the curse of the Yankee nation.
That combination will be so bold,
They'll sell the country for British gold!
The commercial class and speculators
Will become a band of vile traitors.
Their plundering greed will have an end,
And th' Yankee nation will need a friend.

The Americans will come to grief
When their navy aids the British fleet.
Oh, havoc, havoc and great slaughters,
American graves in Chinese waters!
Leprosy, cholera then will rage,
And the fearful Asiatic plague.
Th' metropolitan press 'll be bought and sold;
It will become the slave of British gold.
All corporations will come to grief;
They'll be treated as a common thief.
Civilization labor will enthrall,
Then will come havoc and the dogs of war.
The civilization of my own time
Will end 'ere nineteen hundred and ninety-nine!
Woe! Woe! to the administration,
That piles up mountains of taxation!
With foreign wars and imperial sway,
The greatest republic will then decay!
Trusts and syndicates will come to grief;
Their time and term will be very brief.
That party surely will feel the rod,
Who slaughter people in th' name of God.
With sword, famine and conflagration
Teach Christian gospel and salvation.
Woe! Woe! hypocrites, surely you will fall,
Who teach religion with powder and ball.
The sons of Mammon will have a craze,
To grab up land then will be the rage.
You can't do it, for it's all gammon;
You cannot serve both God and Mammon.
Colonization, whatever be th' theme,
Trade and cheap labor surely is the game.
No matter what may be the contention,
To get cheap labor will be th' intention.
The Yankee scheme of colonization,
Will meet the people's condemnation;

For the Americans of all classes
Will yet oppose mountains of taxes.
The people then will surely rant and rave
'Gainst taxes from the cradle to the grave!
The sons of Mammon, say what you can,
Will yet deride th' divine right of man.
In Mammon's temple to have a niche
They'll toil and moil, such will be their wish.
In this free country schemers yet will plan
To nullify th' equality of man.
On th' people's necks will be a heavy yoke
When they abandon the popular vote.
Th' regular army, in all climes and ages,
Has been th' tool of despots and dictators;
Th' regular army, in a fatal hour,
Will overthrow freedom and th' civil power;
Th' regular army with the power civil
Agrees as God does with the devil!
A hireling army, aristocracy—
The source of nobles and of monarchy.
The people of this mighty nation
Should now beware of usurpation;
For usurpers sneak like a thief at night,
For to get power either wrong or right.
The people should beware of King Log,
And the man of destiny King Stork!
And a usurpers' revolution
Will violate the constitution!
Tartars and Turks will fight their battles o'er;
The Russians will take Constantinople.
Ancient nations had their rise and fall,
Oh, England! the "writing is on the wall."
The Russians will enter Samarcand,
And next they will enter Hindostan.
The nations' flags will be unfurled;
England's navy into ruins will be hurled,

2

The news will resound from pole to pole
That Britannia's empire is no more!
England, England, the people you enthrall,
Your kings will downward slide and fall;
God is just—what fearful retribution;
You despots, fear the coming revolution.
Your flag, which brought you power and gain,
Will soon be swept from every main,
And in your harbors, slips and fine docks
Your merchant ships will lie and rot!
The sails of commerce no longer spread,
Now the people starve for work and bread.
Th' busy marts, where flourished wealth and trade,
Show the sad destruction of th' midnight blaze.
Britons who fought for England's renown,
Plunder'd countries and the wealthy town;
England's fleet driven from ev'ry foreign shore,
England's starved millions plunder now at home!
Ah! you who carried war near and far,
Behold the horrors of internecine war.
England, who warred on the world o'er,
Your sons will be your direst foe.
Despotism will surely meet its doom;
Th' conflict 'll be between the rich and poor.
The rich shouldn't forget that wealth and poverty
Hold different views of the rights of property!
Down, down with despots and th' tyrants' rag;
Hail, revolution and freedom's flag.
The Saxons will meet with retribution,
From Latin and Slavic persecution;
The British flag will be swept from the sea;
Then Ireland will be glorious and free.
What great rejoicing from pole to pole,
The Saxon power will be no more.
To rule the world now is England's aim;
Like Rome, she will fall of her own weight.

England's colonies over the sea
Will be republics—the people free;
England will be coop'd in her island home,
Forever and forever—ever more!
Th' New Zealand traveler 'll behold with awe
From London bridge the ruins of Saint Paul's.
In one great battle th' trumpet will resound,
And England's forts will be as Danish mounds.
Then England's fall and devastation
Will make Ireland a glorious nation.
The Irish republic will take its station
Among the most enlightened nations.
Oh, Erin's son, thou art not forgot,
Emmet's epitaph is writ at last!
Heed you this moral, all true Irishmen,
Believe in prophecy and Columbkille.
Let the watchword now and ever be,
That all nations must and shall be free!
Ease and luxury will cause disease,
And filth from sewers will breed the plague
Th' dirt of cities and many a town
Into the rivers will pour down.
The rivers will flow to the ocean tide;
Plague and malaria they'll leave behind.
Th' Mississippi 'll be a disease breeder,
Malaria, plague and yellow fever.
Th' American people will come to woe
When they abandon th' doctrine of Monroe.
When they take "spoils"—indemnification,
Woe! Woe! to the American nation.
Th' monarchs of Europe will set a trap,
And with our own coin will pay us back!
Th' American people in God may trust,
'Till they get avaricious and unjust.
Workingmen will meet dire starvation
From Japanese and Chinese immigration.

American blood will be tainted
With the blood of Asiatic races;
From the immigration of all races,
Americans will have yellow faces.
And of all races from foreign land,   *
Th' Malay pirates will be the worst brand.
The Filippinos will cause great woe,
And prove to be our most deadly foe!
Syndicates will yet devise a plan,
To tropical climes they'll move their plant.
Where slaves, boors, serfs and coolie labor
Will work for mere starvation wages;
And under the American flag,
Th' produce of cheap labor they'll bring back;
The American market they will flood
With coolie cheap-labor, ready-made goods.
And it matters not what may be their theme,
To get cheap labor sure will be their scheme.
Like Goths' and vandals' devastation,
Will come a coolies' immigration.
An Asiatic fierce invasion
Will crush th' white man's civilization.
In the name of commerce—foreign trade—
Plunder and land grabbing will be th' rage;
And Americans will rue the day
That they bought land in the China sea;
And their title deed to maintain good
They will lose money and precious blood.
In the Pacific, where Britons sail,
There war will follow for commerce's sake!
In the conflict for trade and power,
England's Indian empire will go down.
Oh! England, England, you should beware
Of that great power, the northern Bear!
To India will come an invasion—
Cossacks, Russians and Tartar barbarians!

In the Pacific isles th' Polynesians
Will disappear with th' white man's invasion;
War, famine, disease and conflagration
Will follow th' white man's civilization.
Greed, commerce and business knavery
Will promote disguised slavery.
Canting hypocrites will rant and rave,
And will claim it th' work of God and fate.
Mammon's sons, in their hateful greed,
Will claim it the work of Christ's holy creed.
The forced labor of all creation,
Is Mammon's creed and civilization.
The Oceanicans, sad to relate,
Extermination sure will be their fate.
Trade and commerce will be Mammon's theme;
Disguised slavery sure 'll be th' scheme.
And some Christians will join Mammon's clan,
And will make war on their fellow man.
Pro bono publico—"for the public good"—
Will be disregarded—not understood!
Woe to th' vanquished, is the coming theme;
The Jew, pagan, Turk, Christian—all the same.
Conquering armies will yet run mad,
Like demons, furies—the scourge of God!
And Mammon's greed and devastation
Will end with the world's conflagration!
The Africans of every creed
Will be made slaves of Saxon greed.
Americans will have a selfish craze,
To get Philippino lands will be the rage.
And some high tariff agitators
Will speak for England and free traders;
They will drink toasts to England and Queen Vic,
And for land and commerce, that of old Nick!
Some Americans 'll act like an ape,
And our ambassadors at St. James

Will dance attendance—sad my story—
.They will act the sycophant and toady.
Some drunken lords, with laughter and jeer,
Our toady ambassadors will cheer.
Juan Toro is sometimes quite civil
When full of French wine after dinner.
Juan Toro knows that the Yankee nation,
Of all th' world, is a conglomeration!
But he claims them as his blood relation,
For the sake of trade and for taxation.
Juan Toro has humor, schemes and trick,
He knows that a lie well told oft 'll stick.
When drinking wine he has roars of laughter,
When he calls the Yankees Anglo-Saxon!
When the Norman knights were warriors brave,
Th' Saxon swineherd was a villain slave.
Then the Norman knights, with sword in hand,
Fought from the Land's End to the Holy Land.
Writers, speech-makers, when you wine and dine,
'Twas Normans fought in France and Palestine.
Britons, Normans, Scotch and Irish braves,
Are you all lost—merg'd in Saxon slaves?
The Britons sure did rue their folly,
When they made the Saxons their ally.
They found, when late, that the Saxon's greed
Is land grabbing, whate'er be their creed.
Britons, when the Saxons they did trust,
Found when late the Saxons are unjust.
The Saxon plan of civilization
Is war, conquest, trade and taxation.   ·
And it matters not what they may pretend,
Selfish people are never a true friend;
And though sometimes they may prove a friend,
Like Satan, they are treacherous in th' end.
Frothy orators of Plymouth Rock,
Why ignore the Irish and the Scotch?

Some Americans are getting funny;
The Saxon craze is religion and money.
Th' "disease of building" will make men insane,
Then people will be "tax-paying slaves."
And then with higher civilization
Will come poverty, crime—taxation!
, The wild birds will have a habitation
In ruins—buildings which cost taxation.
And public buildings which cost a big tax,
Like Rome and Babylon, will yet grow grass.
Churches will be held in pawn or bondage,
Which is another name for mortgage.
For pride, splendor, luxury, waste and greed
Will pervade every nation and creed.
Men will be selfish—in their greed for gain
They will pile on debts for unborn heirs.
The people of all nations yet will rue,
When they'll be in bondage to th' Shylock Jew;
A time will come and Shylock will bewail
The world bankrupt—ah! nobody then will pay!
The time will come when the toiling masses
Will rebel 'gainst interest, debts and taxes.
Shylock will have only his hidden store
Of gold, silver, diamonds, gems, precious stones;
His bonds, notes, securities of all kinds
Will float in the air like a paper kite!
There will be barter, traffic will be slow;
The people must pay their way as they go.
To the usurious Jews will come great woe;
They'll not get interest on their hoarded gold.
Woman suffrage 'll cause domestic strife;
Women then will vote both wrong or right.
War, war—the republic overthrown,
Then woman suffrage will be no more.
And a fiery comet will cross our path;
Like a cradle the mountains then will rock,

And great volcanoes and th' earthquake's shock
Will leave desolation in their track.
Fertile fields and cities of great renown,
The same as Lisbon, will be gulfed down.
Where. streams of lava will cross the plain,
None will live to tell the dismal tale.
And tidal waves will run mountains high,
And towns and great cities will destroy.
From fire and smoke great will be the gloom;
It may perhaps be the day of doom!
What I write I believe it to be true,
And merit I give where merit is due.
It is with sorrow I now relate
What is written in the book of fate.

The place of my nativity—
Moorestown is my native land,
    Parish of Kilfinane;
Limerick County, rich and grand,
    Erin's green dominion.

CUDMORE'S
PROPHECY
OF THE

TWENTIETH CENTURY.

PART II.

When the ancients thought that they were right,
The arbiters were the gods and might.
They appeal'd to Mars to decide the fight,
And the guilty party to put to flight.
Treaty breakers were put under ban,
As accursed by the gods and man.
Schemers and frauds who planned to decoy
Were treated as a villain, thief and spy
For with th' ancients no crime was as great
As that of perjury and punic faith!
A perjured president or king
Is a traitor to both God and men.
He may make stump speeches, rant and joke,
But the fiend mocks him—"Your oath! Your oath!"
For a brief applause, power and pelf,
To the arch fiend he has sold himself.
First a demagogue and agitator,
And ends a tyrant and a traitor!
The man on horseback will yet appear,
And he will disband the volunteers.
Then the usurper will come to grief,

And his time in office will be brief!
I now call a witness,—I will be brief,—
Philip of Macedon and th' Saxon chiefs.
They were all perjurers, treaty breakers
Perfidious villains and vile schemers.
They came as friends to fight in freedom's name,
But land and slavery sure was their game.
I now call a witness just at hand;
England, old England, you take the stand.
The chivalrous Normans and the Gael,
War was their sport and the silvan game.
The stranger shared their bed and board,
Faithfully they kept their word and oath,
But the Saxons came, with fraud and guile,
As treacherous allies to the British Isle!
To expel a hoard of invading foe,
But robbed the Britons of house and home.
The Saxons, who fought for power and gain,
Were slaves and vassals to the hardy Dane.
Saxon freedom had a brief repose,
Next came villanage and the Norman yoke.
The Saxons forsook their martial trade,
And practiced falsehood for filthy gain.
From saving pence as petty dealers
They are now th' greatest merchant schemers.
The high, the low, the young, and hoary,
The Whig, the Liberal and the Tory!

Machiavelian agitators
Started a court of arbitrators,
The Utopian idea of the hour,—
To maintain peace and the balance of power.
Cabals, bribers and secret negotiations
Violated sacred obligations!
Alliances, confederates, public laws
Could not chain ambition and th' dogs of war!

All over the world where Britons sail,
Trade, war and plunder follow their trail.
The old excuse, commerce, barter and trade,
While statesmen are scheming to enslave!
With bibles, bawbles, gunpowder and tricks,
Blood on their hands and scripture on their lips.
While burning towns and sacking a city,
Hypocrites and frauds cry, "What a pity!"
Religion, religion, is their theme,
But trade and slavery is the scheme!
Now the English, Christian, Jew and pagan
Worship mammon's civilization!

Machinery and civilization
Will cause crime, poverty and taxation.
And an inflated prosperity
Will make bankrupts and adversity!
Trusts, combines and great corporations.
Will be the curse of all the nations!
And watered stock and like inflation.
Will be crushed by high taxation.

THE HAGUE CONVENTION.

And the greatest humbug and modern fake
The peace convention at the Hague!
Uncle Sam beware of humiliation
From European courts of arbitration,
England's schemes of procrastination,
And diplomatic prevarication.
English diplomats, as in days of yore,
Are slippery friends and a secret foe!
England's claim of common kindred blood—
She will barter all for England's good.
England's court of arbitration is all sham;
She wants millions of dollars from Uncle Sam.

It has been said (I do believe all right)
That courts and juries always have their price.
A universal court of arbitration
Would be the joke of the ancient nations,
And European courts of arbitration
Will end in cabals and humiliation.
Corruption, bribery and combinations,
Intrigue, ambitions and usurpations!
Confederacies, alliances, what not,
Are a pray to th' wily diplomat.
In th' name of freedom, humanity,
He will play th' tyrant, practice villany.
Diplomats smile, and smile, and seem civil;
With all their smiles they will act the villain.
For their country, right or wrong, is their creed;
It matters not if they can well succeed,—
With bribes, intrigue, promises and lies,
Schemes, deceit, ambiguity and spies,
To the world they may appear honest men;
Their inspiration is from Pluto's den!
And for the great tempter, yellow gold,
How oft Europe has been bought and sold;
The Hague convention 'll end in confusion,
The sword, the sword, and dissolution!
There will be wars, wars,—say what you can,
While on earth there is a living man.
The avaricious, the bad, and bold,
Will sell their country for yellow gold!
There have been bad men—that is no fable,—
Since the days that Cain killed Abel!
There will be wars, injustice, again and again,
Till the world is ruled by angels—not by men!

The London bondholders will yet prevail;
They will tell Uncle Sam: "You pay this claim,
Four hundred million dollars cash in hand,—

Porto Rico, Cuban and Philippine bonds.
Don't repudiate; don't be silly.
We can get the cash from German Billy.
To avoid disputes and much vexation,
We cite you to th' court of arbitration."
It is true,—I'm not ashamed to tell,—
There is always favor down in hell,
But England fears not hell,—Pluto's furies,—
For she is an adept packing juries.
And courts and juries are not always right,
For every man surely has his price!
And in a court of arbitration
England will be th' favored nation.
She has no conscience, she has no scruples,
She will bribe with dollars, franks and roubles.
Spouters, editors, and the like sham,
Rail at our senate and Uncle Sam.
For th' rejection—nonconfirmation—
Of England's court of arbitration,
An orator had the temerity,
To call it "The crime of the century!"
Perhaps he was a mere agitator,
Who knew little of the law of nations.
A light weight, all words, words, and much jaw,
Who knew little of the courts and law,
Some people practice fraud and deceit,
And some are full of their own conceit.
Some people should remember the sham
Which robb'd a president—Tilden, Sam!
That court of partisan arbitrators
Of law and justice were violators.
Beware of England and her diplomat,
Limerick's treaty never will be forgot.
The Hague convention will prove a sham,
And a trap to catch good Uncle Sam,
Uncle Sam 'ill send to th' Hague a noodle

Who will take some swag and Rothschild's boodle.
The Rothschilds will become greedier and bold
For now they want to control the world's gold.
I pity the poor peddling, wandering Jew
Who will soon suffer for the Rothschild's crew.
Sure Uncle Sam will soon rue the day
That he sent to London Johnny Hay,
The story of blood thicker than water
Will cause Uncle Sam both blood and slaughter.
England's plan—forcible annexation—
Will cause Uncle Sam humiliation!
Abraham, Isaac, Jacob— th' story is true—
Proclaimed themselves God's chosen few.
And their seed, breed and generations
Made war on all surrounding nations.
When the Jews forsook their holy law
They became lost sheep and had their fall!
They were conquered by the heathens,
Christians, Mahometans and pagans,
And persecuted on every pretence;
They became sharp peddlers and saved their pence.
And as bankers, goldsmiths, they plied their trade
Usurers, syndicates, th' world now enslave.
The Jews, the Jews of every clime,
At Mammon's word have fallen into line
And Mammon's flag they have now unfurled
And bid defiance to the Christian world.
In Palestine they made a final stand,
And fought the Roman legions hand to hand.
Their patriotism and martial glory
Is only written in ancient story,
And the Jew's gold of every clime
Will be piled up in the British Isle.
The Jews are bold with a face of brass,
They want to nail France on the golden cross.
The Saxon English are very bold,

They want to rule the world with th' Jew's gold
The time is brief—it will come to pass—
Jews 'll crucify people on th' golden cross.
The usurious Jews and tax dodgers
Will be run down like wolves and badgers!
For th' Jews—bondholders—there will be war;
Then will come Great Britain's slide and fall.
The Jews who are the outcasts the world o'er,
In sunny France had their happy home.
And for the sake of a wealthy man
The Jews,—the Jews of every land,—
Lavished their gold; sure it was their plan,
To stir up enemies for noble France!

Dreyfus and his Jewish combination
Will come to grief and humiliation.
Zola, Labori, and their vile crew,
Were the hirelings of the Shylock Jew.
And for the Jew's gold, silver and brass
They would nail France on the golden cross.
The Shylock Jews since the creation
Have been dodgers of taxation.
For mean savings and fraud—they've been spurned.
They are now the great misers of the world.
English sympathy for Dreyfus is due
To the fact that Dreyfus is a rich Jew;
And a poor old Jew with a peddler's pack
Would have no sympathy from Uncle Jack
The Jews show'd their malice—disposition
Trying to boycott the exposition.
Their spite and malice will not prevail,
For merchants want to sell their ware.
And the old story is very trite—
"Don't show your teeth if you cannot bite."
Twice convict'd—once commuted—Jew
Has defenders in the hireling crew.

The British press and their hireling pack
Now bark at France like a beagle pack;
And some Irish journals now rant and rave
While noble Frenchmen fill an Irish grave!
An Irish journal—blasphemer!—
Compares Dreyfus to the Holy Saviour!
He should remember Judas Iscariot
For silver sold his Lord and Master!
It is written of the twelve apostles
That one of th' chosen was an apostate.
This Irish journal hasn't far to go,
For he can apply to "Jingo Joe,"
"Jingo Joe," th' great war agitator,
Has his spies, Castle hacks and traitor.
The Irish little can now rely
On a traitor Castle hack and spy!
Let it be now as in the days of yore,
"A traitor once a traitor never more."
The British press and th' British Tory
Remember France and her days of glory.
Irish Tories, France do now deride;
Remember Limerick and Fontenoy!

Hail, Columbia, you may blush for shame!
Your hireling press France doth now defame;
Your hireling press growl at France with pleasure—
France, which gave you her blood and treasure!
You should now remember the days of yore—
Frenchmen fought from Yorktown to Valley Forge.
Where was Juan Toro with his hireling band?
Fighting freedom with a bloody hand!
Ingratitude, what a shameful thing!
Ingratitude is the nation's sin.
France was our ally in time of need—
France which made Columbia great and free!
The famished Irish and th' oppress'd

Have little favor from th' British press.
And the poor negro, burning at the stake—
There is little pity for the wretch's fate.
African slaves are solely oppress'd;
They will have no gold to bribe the press,
The great blot on civilization.
Is London Press Association.
On the British press none can can now reply—
They tell some truths to invent more lies.
Ah, they are adepts at mean, low tricks—
The truth with falsehood how oft they mix!
England's law courts, spies, and Castle hack—
Thousands of juries oft they did pack.
And a thousand, thousands—a million—
Irishmen were hanged on suspicion!
There was no wail or shriek of distress
From the Tories or the British press.
English law—famine—extermination
Thousands hang'd on "private information."

In the public schools are many a fad.
The greater humbug is the modern pad—
In which scholars scribble with poor light.
That and small print will surely dim th' sight.
Then fond mother's will turn to some quack
Who will say the child wants a magnifying glass.
Examiners 'll be an imposition;
Educated fools will get the position.
Civil service will prove a mockery—
A crib for codfish aristocracy.
Eighteen hundred and ninety Uncle Sam
Had many friends in every clime and land.
American statesmen 'll rue their folly,
They'll be the dupes of their Saxon ally.
The Yankee nation will come to woe
For its alliance with "Jingo Joe!"

Uncle Sam has now th' world's suspicion;
Politicians have wrought this condition,
They will go to grass,—they're going that way;
They are lead by Long and old Johnny Hay.
And soon they will hear the grand alarms;
It will be late to pull in their horns!
Pilling up debts for posterity
Will bring on dire adversity.
Taxpayers grovelling on th' ground will lie;
They will yet rally for to do or die.
The ballot box and long agitation
Will get good officers—legislation!
After the death of Queen Victoria,
England's power will be ancient story.
And it will come to pass—the time is brief—
Sunk in the sea will be the British fleet.

Diamond mines, African golden sand—
The English bondholders will yet go mad—
And England's colonization plan
Will bring a great curse on Uncle Sam,
The English press and agitators
Are sowing discord among the nations;
And the love the wolf has for th' lamb,
Is like England's love for Uncle Sam.
The English press and their imitators
Now make war on German and Latin races.
The English merchants will rant and rave,
For Germany will cut off their trade.
And the British press will scheme and plan
To get Germans to fight Uncle Sam.
But their schemes and plans will not prevail;
They will have their labor for their pains.
The British soldiers—what a slaughter
In Africa and Chinese waters!
For God is just,—that is very true—

They will find their Moscow and Waterloo.
British gold hunters will cause great strife,
In Asia, Africa and Klondike.

. Tory Kipling, Mammon's servile slave,
'Gainst th' Boers and all republics rave
He is Mammon's hireling—a great dastard;
A selfish scribbler and poet aster,
Rudyard Kipling, so goes the story,
A poet aster and a British Tory.
His soul is black, his mind is gory;
He wants Boers' blood and calls it glory.
Tory Kipling will soon be forgot,
And his mere dribbling and Tory rot.
The Tory press, of the Yankee nation
Quote Kipling's twaddle with approbation;
And a poet of everlasting fame,
Will write for liberty and not for gain,
He will not be Kipling,—the man of shame;
He'll write for freedom—universal fame.

British soldiers rush to the slaughter,
To shed Boers' blood you'll have your hereafter.
You enlisted for slaughter in your prime,
Your bones 'll bleach in Afrcia's sunny clime;
And for Mammon's greed and trice cursed gold
You must shed innocent blood from pole to pole.
It is your orders to fight and die;
You must never ask the reason why,
The powers of Europe will yet rally,
And drive the Saxons from the Nile valley!
It is the same now as in days of yore—
He who has the most iron will have the gold.
And England will fall, overwhelmed
In her greed as monarch of the world,
Never, never, will there be such thing

As one language, government, and king!
With war, gold and diplomatic theft
England, never, never will rule the earth!
And just like Babylon, Greece and Rome,
England will fall—fall for ever more.
England's diplomacy will not long prevail,
For the world knows she fights for land and gain.
And her war for humanity's sake—
Now.the tyrant's plea and modern fake!
The Boers' blood to heaven yet will cry;
Women and children's shrieks will pierce the sky,
Then cursed gold,—the truth I now tell,—
Better for England th' gold was in hell,
Soon will come England's humiliation,
And th's British empire's annihilation!

FOR SALE BY

P. J. KENEDY,

No. 5 Barclay Street,
New York.

A PITCHED-BATTLE BETWEEN THE IRISH AND THE DANES.

(In the Reign of King Brian Boru.)

"Let Erin remember the days of old,
  Ere her faithless sons betrayed her;
When Malachi wore the collar of gold,
  Which he won from her proud invader;
When her kings, with standard of green unfurl'd,
  Led the Red-Branch Knights to danger;—
Ere the emerald gem of the western world
  Was set in the crown of a stranger."

GENERAL PATRICK SARSFIELD.

(EARL OF LUCAN.)

DEFENDER OF LIMERICK, A. D. 1691.

"Sarsfield is dying on Lauden's plain!
His corslet hath met the ball in vain—
As his life-blood gushes into his hand,
He says, 'Oh! that this was for fatherland!'
Sarsfield is dead, yet no tears shed we—
For he died in the arms of victory,
And his dying words shall edge the brand
When we chase the foe from our native land."

BRIAN BORU.

KING OF MUNSTER AND MONARCH OF IRELAND, A. D. 1014.

"Remember the glories of Brian the Brave,
   Tho' the days of the hero are o'er;
Tho' lost to Mononia, and cold in the grave,
   He returns to Kinkora no more.
That star of the field, which so often hath pour'd
   Its beam on the battle, is set;
But enough of its glory remains on each sword
   To light us to victory yet."

ROBERT EMMET.
A POLITICAL MARTYR.
Died for Ireland, September 20th, A. D. 1803.

CORMAC.

KING OF CASHEL AND PRINCE-BISHOP OF CASHEL AND EMLEY.

"Oh, for the swords of former time!
 Oh, for the men who bore them,
When arm'd for right, they stood sublime,
 And tyrants crush'd before them;
When free yet, ere courts began
 With honors to enslave him,
The best honors worn by man
 Were those which Virtue gave him.
Oh, for the swords, etc., etc."

IRELAND'S GOLDEN AGE.

(In the Reign of King Brian Boru, A. D. 1000.)

"Rich and rare were the gems she wore,
  And a bright gold ring on her wand she bore;
But oh! her beauty was far beyond
  Her sparkling gems or snow-white wand."

OWEN ROE O'NEILL.

THEOBALD WOLFE TONE.

The founder of the United Irishmen. An Irish patriot and political martyr. An Irish republican. His motto was " Nil desperandum." He died for Ireland, November 19th, 1798.

www.ingramcontent.com/pod-product-compliance
Lightning Source LLC
Chambersburg PA
CBHW021430090426
42739CB00009B/1431